This book belongs to
_____

# Christiano Ronaldo

## By Mary Nhin

This book is dedicated to my children - Mikey, Kobe, and Jojo.

Copyright © 2022 by Grow Grit Press LLC. All rights reserved. No part of this book may be reproduced in any form without permission in writing from the publisher. Please send bulk order requests to growgritpress@gmail.com
Paperback ISBN: 978-1-63731-701-3  Hardcover ISBN: 978-1-63731-703-7
Printed and bound in the USA. MiniMovers.tv

Hi, I'm Cristiano Ronaldo.

I was born on the 5th of February in 1985 in the São Pedro parish of Funchal. I'm the youngest of three siblings.

Our home was small and our family couldn't afford much.

When I was young, I played soccer for Andorinha.

I received jerseys and supplies from the hand me downs my father received as a kit man.

I was very thankful.

I later joined a team called Nacional. However, one day when I was 12 years old, a famous Portuguese team called Sporting C scouted me.

My family and I then moved to Alcochete, so I could join the Sporting Youth Academy.

When I was 14, I got to play semi-professional. I was really excited about it!

My mother even approved of me concentrating on soccer only.

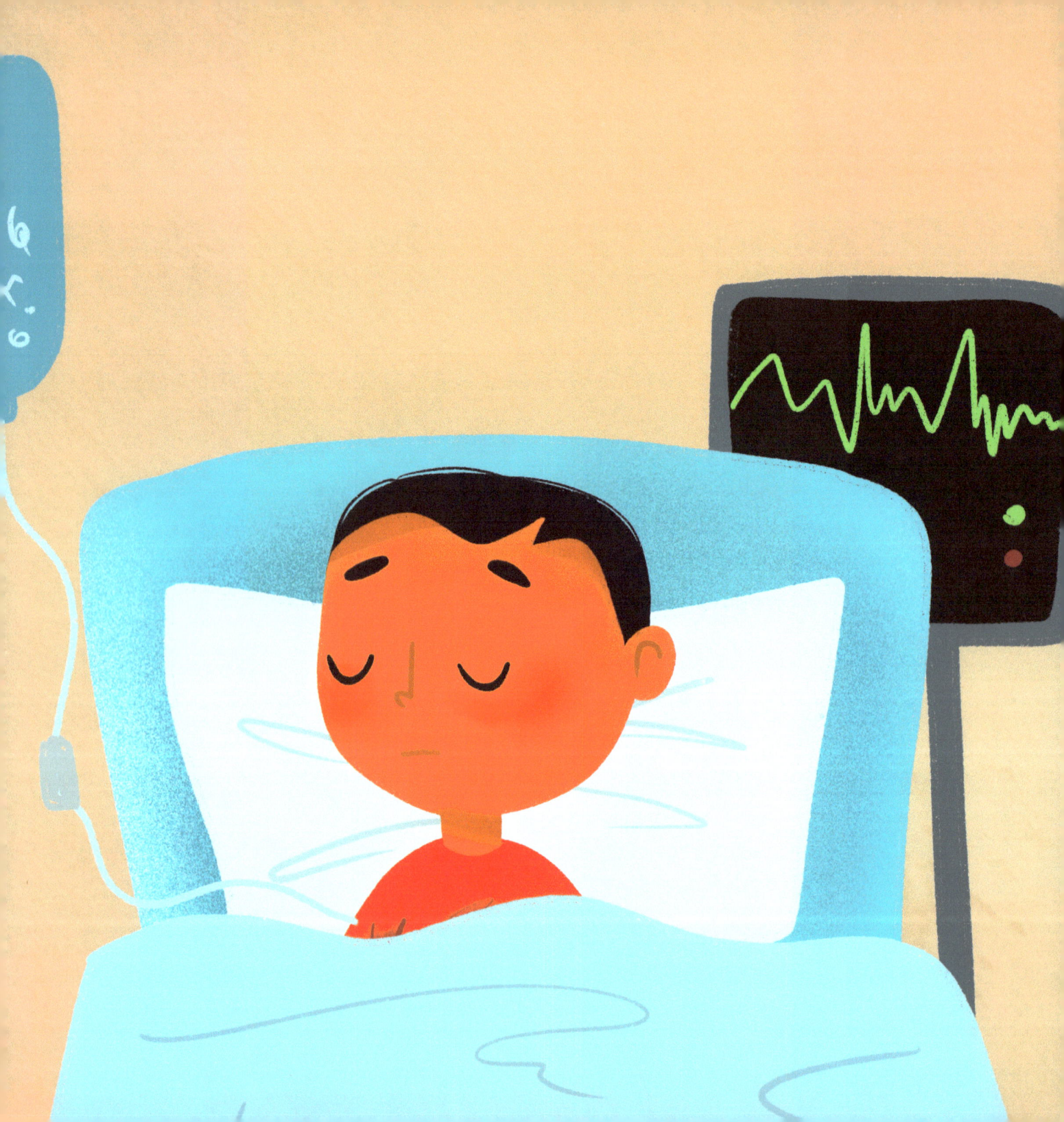

However, my life did not come without challenges.

I was diagnosed with tachycardia. This is a condition that makes my heart rate higher than others when resting. Because of this condition, I almost had to give up on soccer.

I was afraid, but I underwent a surgery that could help my resting heart rate. Fortunately, the surgery was a success and I was able to begin practicing only a few days later.

In 2003, I was able to move to Manchester United, just in time to play against Bolton Wanderers. For my jersey number, I asked if I could be number 28. Instead, I was given number seven.

I received a standing ovation for the game I played against the Bolton Wanderers. However, at times people didn't agree with my playing style. I was getting into disagreements with other players. At the World Cup, I was booed by the audience.

I tried hard not to let the discouragement get to me.

Talent without working hard is nothing.

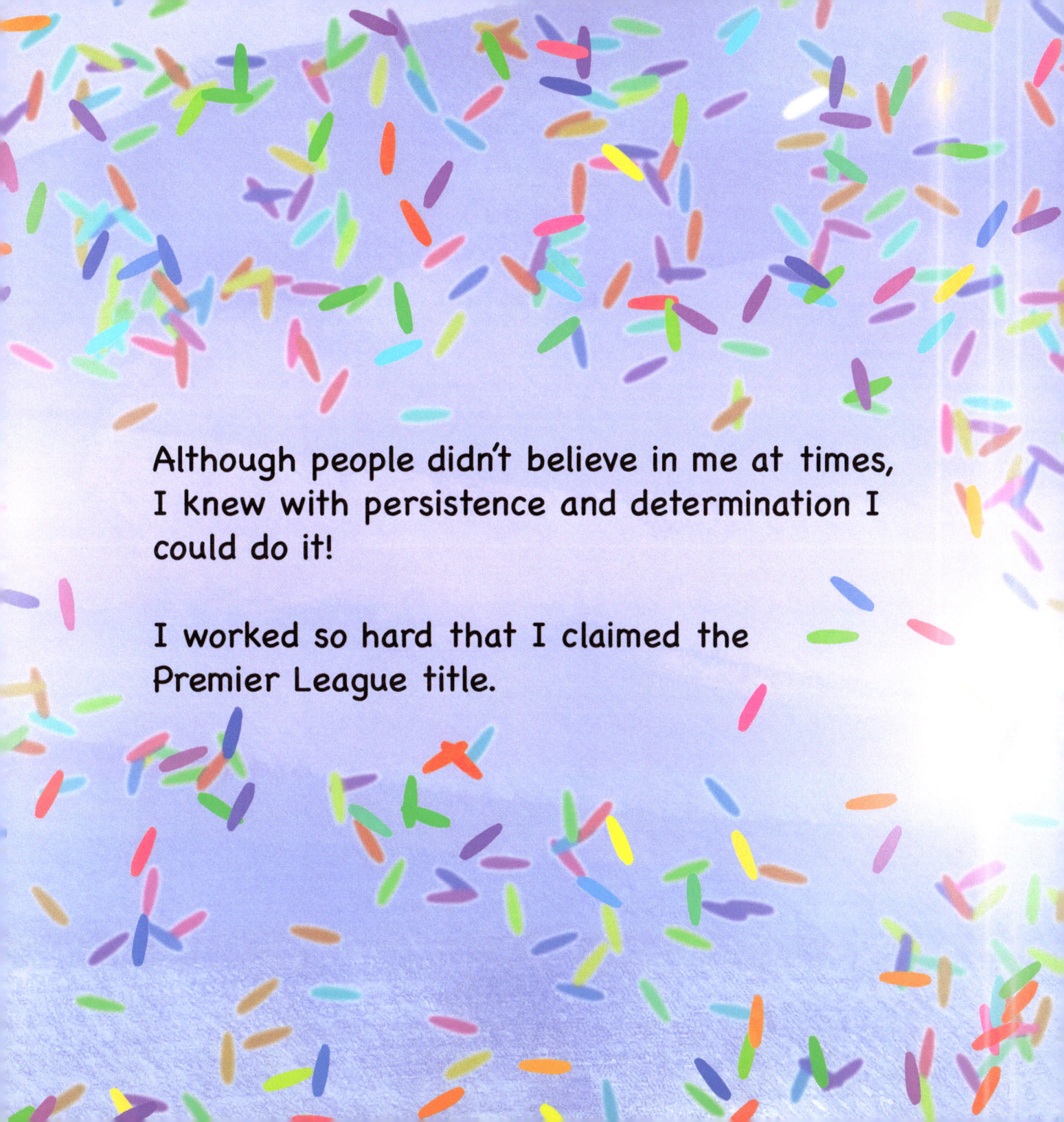

Although people didn't believe in me at times, I knew with persistence and determination I could do it!

I worked so hard that I claimed the Premier League title.

Between 2007 and 2008, I scored 42 goals.

Later, I had to have surgery on my ankle which kept me out of the game for 10 weeks. I didn't let my injury stop me. As soon as I got better, I scored my 100th goal!

In my career, I have achieved many goals I set out for myself, but I couldn't have done it without the support of my loved ones and fans.

I've won five Ballon d'Or awards, four European Golden Shoes, 32 trophies including seven league titles, five UEFA Champions Leagues, the UEFA European Championship and the UEFA Nations League.

I've scored over 800 official senior career goals for my club and country. Currently, I am the only player to score in five different FIFA World Cup tournaments.

I am the first soccer player and the third sportsman to earn over $1 billion in his career.

It's important to me to always give back to the community. I joined FIFA's "11 for Health" program to raise awareness for kids on how to steer clear of drug addiction, HIV, and obesity.

Timeline

1999 - Ronaldo moves to Alcochete

2000 - Ronaldo is diagnosed with tachycardia

2003 - Ronaldo plays for Bolton Wanderers

2004 - Ronaldo helps win the English FA Cup

2008 - Ronaldo is named World Player of the Year

minimovers.tv

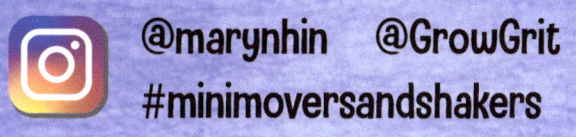 @marynhin    @GrowGrit
#minimoversandshakers

 Mary Nhin    Ninja Life Hacks

 Ninja Life Hacks

@ninjalifehacks.tv

www.ingramcontent.com/pod-product-compliance
Lightning Source LLC
Chambersburg PA
CBHW041522070526
44585CB00002B/48